For Whom the Bell Tolls

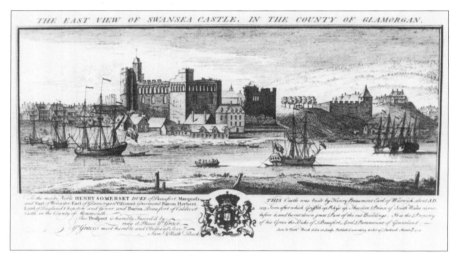

Swansea Castle.   (*Courtesy Swansea Museum*)

For Whom the Bell Tolls

A Century of Executions

Peter J. R. Goodall

First Impression—2001
Second Impression—2001
Third Impression—2005

ISBN 1 84323 022 4

Printed in Wales by
Gomer Press, Llandysul, Ceredigion

*for
my wife Pauline,
my children
Andrew, Wayne and Amanda,
and my grandchildren*

Acknowledgements

I would like to thank the following for their invaluable help in the preparation of this book:

My wife, for her many hours of proofreading; the Home Office who authenticated the material used; the governors and staff of Swansea Prison, many of whom have collected and divulged snippets of useful information over the years, in particular Peter Clatworthy and Mark Arnold; the Rev. Ted Hunt, retired chaplain to the prison, who provided articles from his late father's book, *To Guard My People* (Superintendent W. W. Hunt of the Swansea Borough Police); the staff and reporters of *The South Wales Evening Post*, for encouraging me to pursue publication of this book; the staff of Swansea Public Library and Merthyr Public Library; The Glamorgan Archive Service, Cardiff and Swansea; Steve Fielding, author of *The Hangman's Record*, who provided the profile of the executioners who officiated at Swansea Prison hangings; Professor Meic Stephens for permission to print Harri Webb's poems, 'Cox's Farm' and 'The Hanging of Bob Coe'; Mr Brian White, retired Senior Officer of Gloucester Prison; West Glamorgan Archive Service, Swansea, for the use of the Swansea Tithe Map, and the 1897 Ordnance Survey Map, of which the West Glamorgan Archive Service holds the originals.

Whilst every effort was used to trace the authors of articles used in this book it was not possible in every case. I would be pleased to recieve any information which has necessarily been omitted here.

Peter J. R. Goodall
Swansea, October 2001

Foreword

For those many thousands of people who have lived their lives in our 'ugly, lovely' city of Swansea, the large forbidding building on the foreshore of Oystermouth Road has been a constant reminder of a life apart. Many of us pass by day after day without much thought for the lives of those on the other side of the wall, whilst a minority on both sides of those high forbidding structures are only too aware of the consequences on their lives of incarceration within. The author of this history of the prisons of Swansea is one such individual, as he has served the prison service here as a warden for approaching twenty years.

The 'house of correction' has been a feature of our community for over a thousand years, and until relatively recent times was a focal point of the life of the town, especially at times of execution. For hundreds of years such events were regarded as a public spectacle and often led to rowdy scenes and even riots. During the centuries leading up to the 1830s, the death penalty was meted out for a whole range of offences, from petty theft upwards. Thus the spectacle of a public hanging was a regular occurrence which brought out both the best and worst emotions in the local populace. The extreme public emotions engendered by the recent executions in the United States are an example of what occurred in Swansea on a regular basis up until the middle of the nineteenth century.

From about 1870, executions, which by then were the penalty for murder only, were carried out within the privacy of the prison walls. Nevertheless, they still required the involvement not only of the executioner and his staff but also warders, matrons, chaplains, governors, under-sheriffs and high sheriffs. As High Sheriff of the

County for the current year I am profoundly relieved that I shall neither have to make arrangements for nor witness such a ceremony.

Whatever your personal views on capital punishment and, indeed, on society's response to wrongdoers generally, you cannot deny the importance of the subject, nor the influence that punishment regimes and their methods of enforcement have had on our societies over the centuries. The history of law enforcement in Swansea is very much intertwined with the history and development of the town itself, and we owe a debt of gratitude to Peter Goodall for the time and effort expended to record this aspect of our heritage for current and future generations.

D. Peter L. Davies
High Sheriff of West Glamorgan
for 2001-2002

9

chapter one

The Prison System

SINCE the beginning of time, prisons have played a significant role in protecting society from those who offend against law and order. In the early days, prisons were little more than dark, dank dungeons where poor wretches were thrown, chained to the wall and left to rot. Incarceration without trial was rife, usually at the whim of some unscrupulous overlord.

The situation took a decided turn for the better when, in 1531, an Act of Parliament created a system of common gaols, built in towns where Quarter Sessions were usually held. A further Act in 1699 brought such establishments under central control. Conditions inside the prisons were, however, still appalling for many years to come, and it took great dedication from nineteenth-century reformers such as the renowned Elizabeth Fry to make significant inroads into what remained an abusive system.

Born in Norwich in 1780, Elizabeth Fry was a Quaker who made her first visits to Newgate Prison in 1813 to distribute clothes to the inmates. She then began to campaign for the improvement of conditions within prisons, and established a school inside the prison for the children held at Newgate. Classes were held in one of the cells, and were run by a female convict called Mary Connor.

Transportation of convicted prisoners to the colonies had begun in the sixteenth century, and did not end until 1837, when the Australian colonists objected to the process. The British government was then forced to think seriously about how to deal with hardened criminals. Consequently, in 1839, the Prisons Act made the classification and segregation of prisoners compulsory, and two new systems were introduced. The Separate System kept prisoners totally isolated from one another, apart from brief periods spent in chapel, whilst the Silent System forced prisoners to work in absolute silence at all times.

In 1864, penal servitude was introduced as an alternative to transportation, and new convict prisons were opened. Prisoners were engaged in 'public works' from which the community as a whole would benefit – quarrying stone, building roads, constructing quays and breakwaters for dockyards and so on. It was a lucrative business.

Dartmoor Prison Quarry. The Prison Warders were armed with cutlasses or muskets as can be seen in the photograph, (c. early 1900s).
(Courtesy H. M. Prison Service Museum, Newbold Revel)

Accounts of Thomas Lewis, gaoler, 1760

To the expense of executing Francis Rosser

for murder, paid to the hangman. £4..4..0

Paid for ale punch and vitals for

the above. £0..15..0

Paid for horse and cart to haul

him to the gallows. £1..0..0

Paid for halter. £0..0..6

For horse and cart to haul his

body to Neath to be in chains. £4..0..0

In 1871, prisoners from Portland, Portsmouth and Chatham earned £149,000 between them, and as a result, the cost of operating the three prisons that year was a mere £131,000.

The final years of the nineteenth century saw considerable debate about the running of prisons. Although the principle of segregating juvenile offenders from their adult counterparts had been put into practice through the establishment of a series of Reformatory Schools after 1854, it was not until the Children's Charter of 1908 that full segregation was brought about.

In the case of adult prisoners, the authorities tended to favour the Separate System, which was in effect solitary confinement. It was thought that, if a prisoner was separated from the bad influence of other criminals and left alone with his thoughts, he could effectively be 'softened up' over a period of months and then influenced by staff and prison chaplains into leading a better way of life. The loneliness of the Separate System, however, drove many men to madness and suicide. It was a system fuelled by fear – fear of being put to hard

Prisoners on a
tread wheel.
*(Courtesy H. M. Prison
Service Museum,
Newbold Revel)*

labour on machines which would now be classified as instruments of torture. Two of the most notorious of these were the tread wheel and the crank.

In 1878, a new Prison Act removed all prisons, whatever their category, from the hands of local authorities and brought them, like the convict prisons, under the control of the Home Office. Yet it took another twenty years for the excessive use of hard labour and corporal punishment to be abolished completely. At the beginning of the twentieth century, for example, there were still thirteen tread wheels in use in British prisons.

The Prevention of Crime Act of 1908 was a revolutionary piece of legislation which, amongst other things, put an end to the cropping of prisoners' hair and the wearing of broad-arrow suits for convicts. It also provided formal training for all prison officers. Then, in 1922, Sir Alexander Patterson's Prison Commission revolutionised contemporary thinking on the subject, arguing that: 'It must be clear from the outset to all concerned that it is the sentence of imprisonment, and not the treatment accorded in prison, that constitutes the punishment. Men come to prison as a punishment, not for punishment.'

The death penalty was in use in our penal system for all of the nineteenth and part of the twentieth centuries. It was not abolished until 1965, when the Murder Act was finally passed. Judges were, by the terms of the Act, given the power to recommend a minimum sentence of life imprisonment whereby all convicted murderers should serve a recommended period in prison before being considered for release. However, it was not until 1999 that the death penalty was completely removed from the Statute Books.

Gloucester Gallows.
(Courtesy H. M. Prison Service Museum, Newbold Revel)

There are many different kinds of modern prisons. In all but minimum security establishments (known as 'open prisons') the task of maintaining the physical custody of prisoners is given the highest priority. At the same time modern prisons offer inmates considerable opportunity for work, recreation, vocational training and education.

New early-release arrangements came into force in 1992 with the old system of remission, release and parole being replaced by one based on the length of the sentence. Now all prisoners serving sentences up to four years are released automatically at the halfway stage. Prisoners serving sentences of four years or more are eligible for parole once they have served half their sentence. Only those who offend against prison rules whilst in custody could have their release date deferred.

The days of penal servitude have long gone. Problems still exist – the prison population is rising and offenders are, it seems, becoming younger and more violent. In the years ahead, the prison service will undoubtedly have to develop new ways of dealing with significant and demanding problems. In the nineteenth and twentieth centuries, however, when the death penalty was still in use, some prisoners' lives were brought to a dramatic and abrupt end at the gallows. This book relates the stories behind the fifteen executions which took place at Swansea Prison between 1858 and 1958.

chapter two

Cox's Farm (Swansea Prison)

THE original prison or gaol at Swansea was located in the town's castle. Built sometime around the year 1113 by Henry de Beaumont, Swansea Castle was attacked many times and was in fact burned down by the warlike Welsh who saw the establishment of a Norman stronghold in their traditional homelands as an infringement of their liberty and freedom.

The earliest written records available note that William de Braose, Lord of Gower, was once in possession of the castle. In his Charter of 1305, de Braose solemnly promised that no burgess of the town would be detained there unless he was a felon or a prison-breaker whose detention had been ordered by a court.

The first recorded 'governor' – although he would not have recognised the title – was Thomas Somer. He was the catchpole for the town (a sheriff's officer) and also a constable, his pay in 1402 being a mere 2d (less than 1p) per day.

Incredible as it might seem, Swansea Castle was still in use as a debtors' prison up to the middle of the nineteenth century, and even at this late date, conditions were extremely grim. However, inmates were at least able to leave the prison during the day in order to sell

Swansea
Castle.
*(Courtesy
Swansea
Museum)*

Castle Lane 1850.
(Courtesy Swansea Museum)

items to make money. In the words of E. Donovan, who inspected the castle in 1805:

They are allowed to expose whatever articles their slender funds may enable them to muster for sale in the open street on that side of the market fence next to the castle. The limit of that bailiwick was distinctively pointed out by a range of small stones down the highway, and within this boundary the debtors are as secure from the molestations of their creditors as though they were confined to their dismal cells within the castle walls.

The use of Swansea Castle as a prison was finally abolished in 1858. By that time the new Bridewell Prison, construction of which began in 1826, had been running for several years.

Opened in May 1829, the Bridewell, or House of Correction, as it was known, stood on land located to the south of the main wing of the present-day prison. The first governor was a man named William Cox. A map of Swansea Corporation, dated 1838, shows that he leased a small part of the land adjacent to the prison and here he grew vegetables and other crops with which to supply the prisoners. From this small piece of land came the name Cox's Farm, and, to this day, Swansea Prison is still known among locals as Cox's Farm.

In 1851, the prison was described as half-octagonal in shape, containing ten wards or cell areas with exercise yards and two main airing yards. Each category of prisoner was segregated and each category therefore used a separate exercise area. There were sixty-two sleeping cells and two infirmaries. The original entrance to the Bridewell faced north, on a road that has long since disappeared under the prison grounds. The first Governors' house was located at that entrance and had a large bay window from where the Governor could observe the activities of the prisoners in the yards.

During the tenure of William Cox – and of his son, William Cox Junior, who succeeded him as governor – the tread wheel was in regular use as a form of occupational therapy. A symmetrical drum, about six feet in diameter, it had rows of steps on its outside surface and worked on the principle that as soon as a man stepped into the drum it would begin to revolve under his weight. He would then have to keep climbing on the spot in order to maintain his position. After a day on the tread wheel prisoners might have travelled as far as 2193 feet per hour and climbed over 9000 feet in total (twice the

Cox's Farm

My uncle kept a public house,
The Glamorgan Arms so neat,
It stood just off the Mumbles Road
At the bottom of Argyle Street,

And when I was a little boy
My Uncle Wil so kind
Would show me the walls of Swansea Jail,
So high and huge and blind.

That's where the wicked people go
To save us all from harm,
So watch your step in life, my lad,
Don't end in Cox's Farm.

It is no rural residence
But a place of dismal fame,
No flocks they keep, no crops they reap,
Its harvest is of shame.

The gasworks stink and the buffers clink
As the shunting trucks go by
And each man stares through prison bars
At a scrap of Sandfields sky.

But the Tree of Liberty shall grow
From that dark and bitter earth
For patriots bold its high walls hold
In the pangs of a nation's birth.

Here's a health to all who've made a stand
To keep our land from harm
And served their spell in a prison cell
And dwelt in Cox's Farm.

Harri Webb

The tread wheel was used as a form of exercise and occupational therapy, but the other form of punishment in use during the period, the crank, was soul destroying. At least on the tread wheel you left the confines of your cell – the crank was in fact *part* of the cell itself. Comprising a large box, fitted to the wall or floor and filled with sand and gravel, it had a large handle similar to an old mangle projecting out of the side. Inside was a paddle which had to be pushed through sand and gravel. The number of times the handle was turned was dictated by the warder. A 'screw' on the side, when tightened, added to the pressure.

The turns on this machine could be set to 10,000 or 12,000 a day. It was usual to make a prisoner perform so many revolutions in order to obtain his meals – 1,000 before breakfast, 5,000 before lunch and so on.

It was from this period that the nickname 'screw' was given to prison warders, who would tighten the screw to make the pressure greater. A Royal Commission in the 1870s discovered that one man had eaten only nine meals in twenty-one days because he had failed to complete the number of turns ordered by the warder.

height of Ben Nevis). The tread wheel at Swansea Prison was still in use at the end of the nineteenth century, when it was used to pump water from the prison's two wells.

The land around the Bridewell was sold to the county in 1850 and work began on the construction of a new prison almost immediately, which still stands today. On 24th June 1856, the public highway which had run in front of the Bridewell was diverted to become the present Glamorgan Street. Together with improvements which had taken place in the old buildings in 1843 and 1848, the new prison was completed and fully operational by 1861. The present C wing is now the only part of the original structure still standing. A bricked-up arch can still be seen at ground level on the west side of the building. This led to a coal-fired boiler house which provided hot water and heating for the self-contained buildings.

William Cox Junior took over as governor on the death of his father in 1843. He himself died on 25th May

1873 at the age of fifty-nine. He died in post as governor not of the Bridewell but of the newly-named Swansea Prison, and was succeeded by Frank Knight.

The signature of William Cox Junior.
(Courtesy Glamorgan Archive Service, Cardiff)

Swansea Prison under construction in 1858. *(Courtesy Swansea Museum)*

Map showing the land adjoining the House of Correction for the construction of Swansea Prison.
(Courtesy West Glamorgan Archive Service)

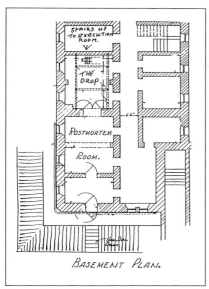

Floor plan dated 1927.
(Courtesy H. M. Prison, Swansea)

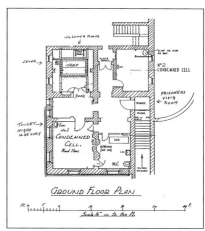

Floor plan dated 1927.
(Courtesy H. M. Prison, Swansea)

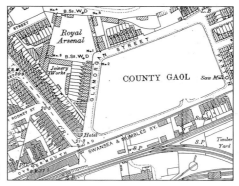

Street map dated 1897.
(Courtesy West Glamorgan Archive Service)

Work on the new Swansea Prison began around 1859, and was completed in 1861. It covered an area of four and a half acres and was designed to hold 166 males and 52 females, although the daily average was about 139 and 34 respectively.

In the north-west corner, in the area which is now the staff car park, there is a bricked-up entrance in the wall. The contractors used this entrance to connect the pipes for the discharge of waste from the prison to Glamorgan Street, and also as a rear works entrance, before finally bricking it up when the work was completed.

By the time it was finally completed, Swansea Prison had five wings. Both men and women prisoners were housed at first, women being held in separate wings. The east wall had no cells or windows, so that women would not be able to catch sight of the men in the other parts of the prison.

A white-bricked hospital block was built in 1898. It was originally a single-storey building but an upper floor was added in 1960. It contained four sick cells, one padded cell and dispensary and, according to local legend, had two of the most beautiful porcelain baths ever seen in south Wales.

The massive stone buildings of the gatehouse face south. The Governor had accommodation on the right, his rooms extending over the gateway. On the left was a three-flat tenement house where the Chief Warder and Chief Engineers were housed. The area where the staff car park is now located was once a tenement in which nine warders and their families lived.

In the early years of the twentieth century the reception area for new male prisoners was in the basement of what was called 'the centre'. New prisoners climbed from the courtyard up wide stone steps and entered the prison via the main door. (This huge oak door still functions today as the main entrance to the prison.) Inside, to the right of the entrance door was the visiting room, which was described as being three-cornered. Once inside the walls, new arrivals descended to the reception area, a part of the prison which was described as being 'dark and ill ventilated'. The gas light always burned in this corridor.

The tread wheel, which, it was stated in a governor's report of 1867, could accommodate sixty-four prisoners at one time, was located in a separate stone building on the north side of the prison. After the tread wheel was abolished, the building was converted into an industrial workshop for a time and, subsequently, it was in this building that the early executions at Swansea Prison took place before a purpose-built execution room was constructed in 1926. On the upper floor of the old Tread Wheel House, a stand beam and brackets for use in executions were built, but there was no trap for the drop: these had to be borrowed from Cardiff Prison. This building was demolished on 24th September 1963 in order to make way for a new classroom and boiler house.

By 1929, however, a purpose-built execution shed was in existence at Swansea. This new execution shed was built onto the old female wing. Detailed plans of the building show the condemned cells, bathrooms and the trap where the executions took place.

Fifteen executions took place at Swansea Prison, between 1858 and 1958, a period of exactly one hundred years. From the passing of the sentence to actual execution, three clear Sundays were allowed – in all, a period of about twenty-one days. The executioner arrived at the prison by four o'clock on the afternoon before the execution and, during the intervening hours, it was his task to set the gallows. He would also consult the prisoner's records to calculate the length of the drop required. If this drop was too long the condemned man would be decapitated; however, if it was too short he would die from strangulation. The rope had to be stretched by the use of sand-bags and would be used only once. It was a much sought after souvenir, often sold by the hangman himself to morbid collectors once the sinister business of the day was over. One

It was not uncommon for the condemned man to put on two stone whilst awaiting execution. This became known as 'grief fat'. When it is considered that most of them were on 'Death Row' only for three Sundays and that their diet was fairly normal prison fare, this was a considerable amount of weight to put on in such a short space of time.

25

hour before the execution the weights would be removed in order to allow some elasticity to return to the rope.

By the beginning of the twentieth century the condemned cell in most prisons was located close to the gallows, thus avoiding a long walk to the execution shed and also undue stress, problems and potential mistakes. Even so, accidents did happen. On 11th December 1928, at Swansea Prison, the assistant executioner (Alfred Allen) failed to clear the trap door when executioner Robert Baxter pushed the lever. Allen followed the condemned man into the pit, albeit without serious harm to himself.

Traditionally, a black flag was flown from the top of the prison on execution day, being unfurled at the moment the condemned man met his end. This practice was ended at Swansea after the execution of Joseph Lewis in 1898, and even the practice of ringing the prison bell was stopped soon after. It was considered too stressful for the condemned man to hear the bell as he walked to the gallows. From this time onwards, the only public sign that the execution had taken place was the posting of a notice on the prison gate. However, even this was brought to an end in 1957.

The last execution at Swansea Prison was that of Vivian Frederick Teed on 6th May 1958, and when he went to the gallows the passing of time was the only indication that the execution had taken place.

Swansea Prison today.

26

The Executioners

The sentence of the court upon you is that you be taken from this place to a lawful prison and thence to a place of execution, and that you be hanged by the neck until you are dead; and that your body be afterwards buried within the precincts of the prison in which you shall be confined before your execution. And may the Lord have mercy on your soul. Amen.

THESE words would have been read out by the trial judge to all prisoners found guilty of the ultimate crime of murder. The wording altered very little over the years and was still in use when capital punishment was abolished in the 1960s.

During the three-week wait between sentence and execution, condemned prisoners had to be closely watched. Some tried to 'cheat the executioner' by committing suicide – in one famous case the prisoner cut his own throat so badly that the doctor considered that to go ahead with the execution would cause unreasonable suffering, both to the officials and to the condemned man. He was granted a reprieve to serve a life sentence.

Once the death sentence had been carried out, the body had to hang on the gallows for an hour, partly in order to dispel rumours about people being buried alive. It was then buried in unconsecrated ground, usually in an unmarked grave under well-maintained lawns.

A number of executioners officiated at Swansea. At the time, all of them would have been well-known figures in British society.

William Calcraft was one of the longest serving executioners on record, officiating at dozens of hangings across Britain between 1829 and 1874. He believed in strangulation, allowing a drop of no more than two or three feet. This was a slow and gruesome process. It was after one of his sickening executions that public hangings were brought to an end in 1867, and all further executions took place inside the prison walls.

The slow strangulation of prisoners in which Calcraft specialised was appallingly cruel, being little better than a stool and a rope under a village tree, but Calcraft himself claimed that he remained unmoved by the executions: 'As soon as I have done it, it goes away from me like a puff of tobacco smoke.' He was eventually forced to retire in 1874, but not before three prisoners at Swansea Prison had gone to meet their maker at his hands.

James Berry was chief executioner from 1884 until 1891, succeeding **William Marwood** who was never

William Marwood, who was chief executioner between 1872 and 1883, demonstrated that it was possible to calculate a man's weight and alter the rope accordingly, so that the neck would be broken and death would be instantaneous. He considered himself an 'executioner'. His predecessor William Calcraft was, he said, 'a hangman'.

called on to work at Swansea Prison. Berry always had serious problems calculating the drop required to kill a prisoner. When executing Robert Goodale at Norwich in 1885, he changed his mind several times about the length of rope needed. Goodale was

half carried, half dragged to the gallows in a state of abject terror, and when officials inspected the body after the event they were horrified to discover that his head had been torn clean off his shoulders.

Berry officiated at two hangings in Swansea Prison.

James Billington (1891-1901) succeeded James Berry to the post of chief executioner. He had two sons who followed him in his unusual trade – **Thomas** and **William**.

Thomas and James Billington both officiated at the execution of Joseph Lewis, which was the last occasion on which the black flag was flown at Swansea.

Henry Pierrepoint officiated at one execution in Swansea Prison. According to Henry, the condemned man (William Foy) ignored the chaplain and smoked a cigarette all the way to the scaffold. The butt was still between his lips when they took the body down an hour later.

John Ellis (1907-1923) was involved in many of the executions at Swansea (also, famously, officiating at the execution of Dr Crippen in 1910). He was always nervous at the scaffold and did not take easily to the job, and this despite the fact that he executed a total of 203 people in his career.

In 1923, at the age of 58 years, Ellis committed suicide.

George Brown assisted at just one Swansea execution, that of Big Dan Sullivan in September 1916.

Robert Orridge Baxter (1915-1930s) was the executioner who nearly ended the career of his own assistant, Alfred Allen, at Swansea Prison by pulling the trap lever before the younger man could get clear of the door.

Alfred Allen (1920-1930s), a sergeant in the Grenadier Guards, had officiated in many firing squads during his time in the service. His near fatal escapade in 1928 was his only execution at Swansea Prison.

Albert Pierrepoint was Britain's most prolific executioner until he retired in 1956. He once asserted that:

> *It is my belief that I was chosen by a higher power for the task which I took up. I operated, on behalf of the state, what I am convinced was the most humane and the most dignified method of meting out death to a delinquent – however justified or unjustified allotment of death may be. The fruit of my experience has this bitter aftertaste; that I do not now believe that any one of the hundreds of executions carried out has in any way acted as a deterrent against future murder. Capital punishment, in my view, achieved nothing except revenge.**

Pierrepoint officiated at four executions in Swansea Prison.

Robert Stewart became assistant executioner in 1950, and chief executioner after the retirement of Albert Pierrepoint in 1956. His only execution as chief executioner at Swansea was that of Vivian Teed in 1958, the last man to be executed at Swansea Prison.

* taken from Albert Pierrepoint, *The Amazing Autobiography of the World's Most Famous Executioner*.

The Executions

Manoeli Selapatana & Panaotis Alepis

Executed 20th March 1858

IN 1858, Swansea was a flourishing port with ships and sailors of all nations crowding into the docks. It was a tough and often dangerous environment. On the night of 16th February 1858 the body of Atanasio Mitrepann, a twenty-five-year year old cook on board the *Penelope*, which was then taking on coal in the docks, was discovered in the canal close to the Strand.

A struggle and harsh words in a foreign language had been heard by two watchmen and

Manoeli Selapatana & Panaotis Alepis
(Courtesy The Cambrian)

Date	Name	Executioner	Comments
20/3/1858	Selapatana & Alepis	William Calcraft	The first recorded public hanging at Swansea Prison
12/4/1866	Robert Coe	William Calcraft	The last public hanging at Swansea
1/3/1886	Thomas Nash	James Berry	The Swansea West Pier Murder
10/4/1889	Thomas Allen	James Berry	The Gloucester Hotel Murder
30/8/1898	Joseph Lewis	James & Thomas Billington	Convicted of murdering the Margam Gamekeeper
8/5/1909	William Foy	Henry Pierrepoint & John Ellis	The Mountain Ash Murder
14/12/1911	Harry Phillips	John Ellis	The Gower Murder
6/9/1916	Daniel Sullivan	John Ellis & George Brown	Murder in Dowlais
11/12/1928	Trevor John Edwards	Robert Baxter & Alfred Allen	The Cynon Valley Murder
4/8/1949	Rex Harvey Jones	Albert Pierrepoint	Together with Robert Mackintosh, double execution in one day
4/8/1949	Robert Thomas Mackintosh	Albert Pierrepoint	As above
19/4/1950	Albert Edward Jenkins	Albert Pierrepoint	The Pembroke Murder
28/4/1954	Ronald Lewis Harries	Albert Pierrepoint & Robert Stewart	Murder in Carmarthenshire
6/5/1958	Vivian Frederick Teed	Robert Stewart	The last execution at Swansea

when a loud splash disturbed the night a few moments later, they hurried to the spot. By the light of a lantern and using a boat hook, the men were able to pull a body out of the water. Mitrepann was dead. He had numerous wounds on his body and his head was beaten almost to a pulp.

A sling shot, consisting of strong rope and a ball of iron, about two pounds in weight, was found on the canal bank, and it was assumed that this was the weapon which had caused such terrible injuries to the dead man's skull.

Enquiries were carried out and it quickly became clear that Mitrepann had gone that evening, together with two Greek sailors – Panaotis Alepis, aged twenty-three, and Manoeli Selapatana, aged twenty-eight – to a dancing house known as Powell's Arms in High Street. Alepis and Selapatana had recently arrived in Swansea, looking for a berth on one of the vessels in the docks. One of them had been seen wearing a plaid cap similar to one found on the canal bank.

The events which followed were later recounted in *The Cambrian* newspaper:

> *The two men were seen to enter their lodging house, the* Jolly Tar *in Wind Street, some short time after nine o'clock on the night in question. One immediately ran out of the back of the house and washed out a pocket handkerchief which afterwards he threw upon a jack before the kitchen fire to dry, and this handkerchief had several spots upon it, supposed to be blood.*

The two Greeks were arrested on the same night, within an hour of the murder. The cause of the quarrel was never clear but it was supposed that drink had a large part to play in the fracas. The high moral tone of the report in *The Cambrian* – not to mention its inherent racism – seem hard to believe from our contemporary perspective:

Calcraft, the Public Executioner, arrived at Swansea from London by the quarter past eight train last night. There was a very large crowd of people assembled at the railway station in order to catch a glimpse of a man whose 'Profession' has made him so notorious. He, however, stepped into a fly [a single horse and carriage] and was at once hurried to the gaol where he slept during the night.

The Cambrian, 20th March 1858

For the credit of Englishmen, aye Welsh too, we're glad to be able to say that the persons implicated in this atrocious act are foreigners, Greek sailors, whose long-bladed knives carried as daggers behind their backs make every English heart shudder at the very sight and which are too often drawn and used on the slightest provocation.

Alepis and Selapatana were found guilty of murder and were sentenced to death. The day set, 20th March 1858, was one of bright sunshine, with a cloudless sky. The scaffold was erected to the southwest of the prison, on the sand dunes about 250 yards outside the walls. An immense crowd of between 18,000 and 20,000 people – 'street arabs' (homeless children), women with babies and what *The Cambrian* called 'labourers, carpenters, engineers and mechanics of every grade and description' – arrived to witness the execution.

The condemned men had retired at eight o'clock the previous evening, but from midnight onwards they had been preparing themselves. They had eaten nothing, remarking that food would be superfluous, but had frequently smoked their pipes – a luxury which had been allowed to them by the prison authorities.

At twenty to eight in the morning, prison officials entered the

34

condemned cell, and the executioner Calcraft strapped the men's hands behind their backs. The party then walked calmly to the scaffold. In the words of *The Cambrian*:

> *Up to this time the men had been screened from the immense multitudes gathered in front of the gaol but now they mounted the drop and met the gaze of that vast crowd, still they were unawed by the light of those 18,000 upturned faces, themselves the object of attraction.*

As soon as the condemned men appeared a subdued murmur ran through the crowd, but there were no cries or screams or outbursts of anger. The two men joined hands for a moment and Calcraft shook their hands. As a distant clock tolled eight, the bolt was drawn and the two Greeks fell to their deaths:

> *Alepis seemed to die almost without a struggle, but with his unfortunate companion Selapatana it was different. He heaved violently for some six or seven minutes, but neither required that the executioner should pull their legs in order to shorten the miserable existence.*

Following the execution, the crowd quickly and easily dispersed, even though the bodies were left to hang for a further hour. The scaffold was then speedily removed, leaving no sign of the tragedy which had just occurred.

Robert Coe   *Executed 12th April 1866*

The last public execution at Swansea was that of Robert Coe, who was hung on the dunes outside the prison on Thursday 12th April 1866. It is clear from *The Cambrian*'s report on the event that the debate about public executions had been raging for some time:

> *We are far from believing that any salutary effect is produced upon the minds of the spectators by the exhibition presented them by seeing a poor wretch deliberately and PUBLICLY strangled, and would gladly welcome the alteration in the law . . . by which the criminal should be executed within the precincts of the prison.*

The Cambrian did not question the justice of the execution, however, declaring that: 'if ever a murderer deserved death, surely such a man was Robert Coe'.

Robert Coe was just eighteen years of age, a native of the Midlands who was working in Wales as a striker in a blacksmith's shop at the Powell Dyffryn works. On 2nd September 1865 he murdered his friend and fellow worker John Davies in Graig Dyffryn Wood at Mountain Ash. In his confession, Coe later said:

> *He (Davies) asked me on the way 'What do you want with the hatchet?' I answered 'To cut a walking stick.' When we had been in the wood about a quarter of an hour, and had gone some distance from the hedge, I struck him a blow from behind on the back part of the head with the pole of the hatchet. He fell backwards without speaking a word. I immediately gave several strokes on his neck with the edge of the hatchet until his head was severed from his body.*

The body of John Davies was hidden in the woods and not discovered for several months, although there was a great deal of suspicion and surmise in the town. Davies' father, George Davies, made enquiries about his missing son and, gradually, Coe became implicated. He had been seen drinking with Davies in the Cefn Pennar Inn on the day of the murder and then talking with him at a stile which led to Graig Dyffryn Wood.

Robert Coe had borrowed the murder weapon from a man called Swan. He never returned the hatchet, although it was later found in Swan's house, without him ever knowing how it came to be back there. When examined, blood was found on the fibres of the wood. Coe was clear about his motives:

> *I tied his legs with rope-yarn and took money from his pocket which amounted to 33 shillings [£1.65]. I had no other motive whatever for killing him but a desire for obtaining his money.*

At the time of his arrest and trial, Robert Coe denied the murder – it was only later, just prior to his execution, that he confessed to his crime.

It was widely thought at the time that Coe had gone to America, but he had in fact crossed the valley and was in hiding in Newbridge, pictured right.

The following poem appeared in the columns of *The Cambrian* on 12th April 1866:

O 'tis a fearsome sight to see
That pale wan man's acute agony,
The glare of his wild despairing eye
Now bear upon the crowd, now upward to the sky
As though were straining in doubt and fear
The path of the spirit's unknown career.
Those pinned arms, those hands that ne'er
Shall be lifted again, not e'en in prayer,
That heaving chest — enough 'tis done,
The bolts withdrawn; the spirit's gone
For weal or for foe is known but to ONE.

The date of Coe's execution was set for 12th April 1866. Thousands of people poured into Swansea to witness the event:

> *By the Wednesday evening it gave the appearance of some public rejoicing or festive sport taking place instead of the solemnity which should characterise the proceedings. A considerable number of them who arrived in our town to witness the sad sight were women with infants in their arms, fathers leading young boys, even cripples who could scarcely walk.*

The gallows was erected the night before the execution, in the same spot where the two Greek sailors had been hung eight years before. According to *The Cambrian*, however, events were not quite so orderly this time:

> *The usual collection of showmen set up their stalls and it was said that some drove their carts right up to the gallows and removed their wheels,*

which were then hidden so that the police could not move them on next morning. They then charged a fee to witness this execution from the carts.

By seven o'clock on the morning of the execution a crowd of about 15,000 was waiting outside the prison. Robert Coe was calm and controlled. During the previous three weeks he had spent most of his time studying the scriptures and rediscovering some of the faith which he had held in childhood but had since lost. He walked calmly with Calcraft, the executioner, and other officials to the gallows. *The Cambrian* reported the grave event as follows:

> *As soon as the wretched man made his appearance upon the drop a subdued murmur was heard to run through the crowd, with one or two shrieks or cries from women . . . Four women armed with knives climbed the gallows platform as if to attack the condemned man, and they had to be forcibly removed by the police. In the swaying crowds women and children were trampled underfoot and 120 injured.*

The prison chaplain read the burial service and a number of texts and scriptures. He

Letter from Robert Coe, the Mountain Ash murderer, written to the father of the victim.

Mr George Davies
Dear Sir
    I feel it is my duty to write a few lines to you, as I am the murderer of your son, John Davies. You cannot but think how deeply I regret that I ever should do such an act, and especially to John, as we were companions. But it was the devil working within me that caused me to have such thoughts in my head as to go and kill your son. But you can be sure that I had nothing against him. What is in the papers about John wanting to keep company with the same girl as I did is not true, as I don't think John did know her. But nevertheless I have done a great wrong. But I hope you won't have any ill feelings against my relations, as they do all feel greatly for you. But I must conclude, hoping to meet you all in Heaven. May God grant it? Amen.

Robert Coe,
Swansea.

The Hanging of Bob Coe

The Lower Duffryn colliers
Had got their fortnight's pay
And two of them sat drinking
At the end of a summer's day.

Two friends who worked together
And often spent time so:
John Davies was the blacksmith,
His striker Bob Coe.

Full thirty shillings
Such hardy lads could win,
But that was the last of their spending
At Cefn Pennar Inn.

They'd both sailed to America,
The valley gossip said,
But Coe skulked in the Rhondda
While Davies lay stark dead.

In the woods of Ynys Gwendraeth
His headless corpse was found
By John, the Ton Coch shepherd,
All bloody on the ground.

And in Rhondda they remembered
Who'd been asking all the time
About news from Cynon valley,
And had there been a crime?

Had a body been discovered?
He always wished to know;
They remembered, they reported,
His conscience caught Bob Coe.

He made a full confession
That only simple greed
For the blacksmith's fortnight wages
Had brought him to the deed.

For thirty silver pieces
On the gallows he must stand,
The last to be hanged in public
In the history of our land.

That day the Cynon valley
Was still and silent quite,
They'd all gone down to Swansea
To see the dreadful sight.

As he uttered his repentance
His voice was clear and calm,
Before a crowd of thousands
At the gates of Cox's Farm.

We still speak of that murder
A hundred years ago,
And the blood in Ynys Gwendraeth
And the hanging of Bob Coe.

Harri Webb

40

concluded with The Lord's Prayer and as the words 'Thy will be done' were spoken, the bolt was withdrawn and Robert Coe, the Mountain Ash murderer, plunged into eternity. He died almost immediately and without a struggle.

Whether or not the scenes at Coe's execution were instrumental in ending public executions will never be known. Such spectacles did soon come to an end, however, and Robert Coe has the dubious distinction of being the last man to be publicly executed in Swansea.

The following letter from Robert Coe's father (who shared the same name as his son) was sent to the Mountain Ash murderer when he was awaiting his execution in prison:

My dear Robert,

I write you but I find it hard work. I must say that my grief is more than I can express. I wish to impress upon you that you pay every attention to your spiritual advisor, and if you are guilty of the crime you are now charged with, for the sake of your own soul, for my sake, confess firstly to your very kind Chaplain. I am thankful to hear that you are preparing for a solemn change. Cast thy burden upon the Lord and He will sustain thee.

I am sorry to say that I am so unwell, but I find that God's Grace is sufficient to support me. I can write no more. I now, in the sight of God, for your dear brothers and sisters and your mother and your afflicted father, say farewell. May God prepare us all to meet in Heaven. Amen.

Robert Coe

Thomas Nash   *Executed 1st March 1886*

Thomas Nash was a labourer employed by Swansea Corporation. As a widower, he was unable to care for his two daughters, aged six and seventeen years, and so he lodged them with a Mrs Eliza Goodwin of Plasmarl. This was a fairly common arrangement in Victorian Britain, when children were often placed out with other families.

Nash, however, had fallen behind with his payments and, despite repeated requests, failed to give Mrs Goodwin the money he owed.

Consequently, on the evening of Friday 5th December (Friday being pay day for the Corporation) she brought Martha Ann, the youngest daughter, to the Town Hall. She said later:

> I showed him my bill; it amounted to £1. 16s. 2d (£1.81) for the food of the children up to that day. I gave him the bill and I said, 'here is your daughter; take charge of her. He took the girl; he was then standing in the yard and he said 'I'll come up tomorrow Miss Goodwin, and pay you.'

Nash went almost immediately to the beach and was next seen by some boatmen walking along Swansea pier, holding the child by the hand. It was a wild night, waves were crashing over the pier and the boatmen were suspicious. A few minutes later the man returned without the child and, rather than pass the boatmen, leaped over the rail onto the sand. *The Cambrian* tells us what happened next:

> The men now raised the alarm and ran around to the sands and on coming up with Nash, asked him what had become of the child they had seen in his hands a few minutes before. First he said he had left her on the pier, then that she was under the pier, and then that she had complained that she was tired and wished to be carried. That he had placed her onto the rails to get her onto his back and that she had fallen into the sea.

Nash was taken to the police station, pending enquiries. At seven o'clock that night the body of the child, Martha Ann was found washed up on the beach.

Thomas Nash was brought to trial at Cardiff Assizes, where a packed courtroom waited to hear the evidence and verdict. Found

The following letter appeared in The Cambrian *on Friday 26th February 1886 and was a reply to the proposed reprieve of Thomas Nash:*

To the Editor,

Sir,

I wonder did any of the good people who signed their names to the documents, which were in the lobbies of the chapels on Sunday, for the reprieve of Thomas Nash, think of what they were doing? Or was it that their feelings were rendered tender by the appeals of mercy, which was made by the pastors? Do they remember on a dark, cold, stormy December night, this man (if he can be called a man), deliberately took his daughter by the arm and walked slowly to the bottom of the pier and there threw her into the foaming water beneath? It is their duty to look deeply into this matter and say 'here is a man who murdered his child by throwing it into the sea. It was not in the moment of anger, but he seemed to have had the motive in his head as soon as the child was delivered into his care, and afterwards took her to the pier, and drowned her'. The people of Swansea must not be so good as to forgive everyone who commits a murder, or we shall be getting a very large number of murders here. They must think of justice; they must do justice to everyone. If a man commits a murder, let him hang for it, as a warning to others. I hope people will not think me very harsh, but justice ought to be done. Christian England and Wales must not be the scene of murders, all because she is forgiving.

I remain, yours &c,

A Lover of Justice

guilty of the wilful murder of his own daughter, little account seems to have been taken of the man's state of mind at the time, and the sentence of death was duly passed. His only comment was a brief 'I am not guilty, sir.'

Efforts were made to reduce Nash's sentence to penal servitude for life, in view of his apparently distressed state of mind and also the fact that nobody had actually seen him throw his daughter into the sea. Petitions were deposited in the lobbies of the chapels and churches of the town, but it seems that they were not well supported. When the following letter was received from the Home Office it was clear that the sentence would be carried out:

Llangyfelach Church, where Martha Ann Nash is believed to be buried.

Sirs – With reference to the memorial forwarded by you on behalf of Thomas Nash who is now under sentence of death. I am directed by the Secretary of State to inform you after a careful consideration of all the circumstances in this case he is unable to discover any sufficient ground to justify him advising any interference with the due course of the law.

I am, sir,
Your obedient servant
Godfrey Lushington.

To the last, Thomas Nash was resigned to his fate. Apart from Sarah, his surviving daughter, he received no visitors and seems to have been totally deserted by everyone. At his trial it had transpired that Nash had very recently married for a second time, but his new wife did not attempt to communicate with him in any way following his imprisonment.

The morning of Monday 1st March 1886 found four inches of snow covering the town of Swansea, and the weather was bitterly cold. Only one man, calmly smoking a pipe, stood in the road outside the prison as the sun rose – a far cry from the thousands who had

44

formerly gathered there for the public hangings. *The Cambrian* reported that

Stocks at the former H. M. Prison Service Museum, Leyhill.

> *about seven minutes to eight, after the chaplain had left the condemned man's cell, Berry, the executioner, entered it with the pinioning straps in his hands . . . A broad leathern strap went around the culprit's breast and arms, and was buckled so as to keep his arms to his sides. His hands were clasped in front. Before he was fastened he lifted a forefinger to his forehead in token of obeisance to the Sheriff and the Governor, and looked around once at the warders and others who stood in the corridor outside.*

A letter from Mrs Moira Wiggins which appeared in The Evening Post *in September 2000:*

I remember my late mother, who would have been ninety-eight this year, singing a ditty which went something like this

> Thomas Nash is lying down in Swansea Jail
> For drowning his little daughter, her name was Martha Jane.
> He threw her in the river on a stormy night
> And now she's up in Heaven with the angels bright
> So clap your hands, he's going to be hanged,
> Clap your hands, he's going to be hanged,
> Clap your hands, he's going to be hanged
> Early on Monday morning.

My mother had heard her mother singing this to her when she was a child, which would tie in with the year 1886 when my mother was a young woman. There may have been other verses but this is the only one I know.

It was a short walk to the execution hall, across the open yard which was covered with pure white snow. Nash uttered one brief phrase – 'Lord have mercy on my soul' – then the trap was pulled and he fell six feet into the pit.

A crowd of about 4,000 had eventually assembled outside the prison, waiting for the black flag to be unfurled. The sight was greeted by applause and a few tears, mainly from the women. Within a few moments, however, snowballing had become the order of the day and the dreadful fate of Thomas Nash was forgotten.

Two last-minute confessions by Nash confirmed the justice of the verdict. His reason for the crime was simple – 'I had not told my [second] wife I had children.'

Thomas Allen   *Executed 10th April 1889*

The execution of Thomas Allen in April 1889 caused a great stir in Swansea, partly due to the nature of the crime and partly due to the fact that the condemned man was a Zulu from South Africa. Allen never denied killing his victim, Frederick Kent. However, as he said in a letter to the grieving widow, 'I did not intend to kill your boss'.

On the evening of 18th February 1889, Allen had been on a drinking spree for some hours before staggering out from a public house. On the pavement he met a girl with whom he walked towards the Gloucester Hotel. She told him to go to a certain room and said that she would follow him shortly. He found the room and waited – the girl did not appear. Hearing the occupiers of the room, Mr and Mrs Kent, approaching, Allen threw himself under the bed. In the words of *The Cambrian*, Allen claimed that:

If Mr Kent had looked under the bed and discovered him he would have told him exactly how he got there and gone away quietly, but he was not discovered, and went to sleep under the bed. In the morning he awoke and did not quite remember where he was. He struck a match to see, and with that Mr Kent jumped out of bed and struck him. If he had only spoken quietly to him he would have explained and gone away.

Quite why Allen was in Mr and Mrs Kent's room has never been fully explained. Was he waiting, as he claimed, for a sexual encounter? Or was robbery his motive? The prosecution played heavily on this last possibility as, if robbery was the motive and it resulted in violence, then a conviction was far more likely.

Violence certainly erupted in the bedroom. A revolver was produced and Allen stabbed Mr Kent with a razor – not once, but three times. Mrs Kent managed to get hold of the gun and fired it at the intruder, wounding him in the thigh.

Allen denied that robbery was his motive. His first action, on waking, he said, was to strike a match – something he would certainly not have done had he been intending to steal from the Kents. The jury was not impressed and, after only a few minutes' consideration, returned a verdict of guilty. The sentence of death was then given.

Attempts were made to gain a reprieve and it seems that Allen was quite confident that this would be granted. Public opinion, however, was against him. As *The Cambrian* asserted:

The circumstances of the tragedy enacted on that peaceful Sabbath morning in February will not soon be forgotten. Naturally, they gave rise to a great outburst of horror and indignation, and while the murderer was the object of public execration, deep regret was felt at the untimely end of his unfortunate victim, who was universally respected, and much admiration was expressed at the heroism of his plucky wife, who wounded seriously her husband's assailant.

The news that there would be no reprieve was broken to Thomas Allen on the morning of Tuesday 9th April. The executioner, James Berry, arrived that same day, having performed an execution in Dublin on the previous Monday. He examined the scaffold at the end of the exercise room and tested the trap before judging the weight of the condemned man and working out the length of drop required.

Wednesday 10th April was a beautifully fine day, and as early as seven o'clock in the morning small knots of people had gathered in Oystermouth Road, waiting for the black flag to be hoisted. As the time of execution approached, the crowd swelled to about 2,000 in number, all standing quietly in the sunshine.

When the execution party arrived at the scaffold, Allen indicated that he would like to say something. *The Cambrian* later reported that:

> *The following words proceeded in a choked voice from his lips, 'Lord Jesus receive my spirit this day. Lord Jesus receive my soul.' These words were no sooner out of the wretched man's mouth than Berry stepped on*

one side, and then grabbed the iron lever of the drop. Instantaneously, the bolt slid out, the trap gave way, and the criminal fell into the pit.

The black flag was hoisted at eight o'clock, and was met with cheering from some of the young boys gathered outside.

There was considerable debate in the local press about the death penalty after Allen's execution, and yet it was to be another hundred years before it was finally abolished in Britain.

Leg and arm stocks prevented the prisoner from sitting down. *(Former H. M. Prison Service Museum, Leyhill)*

Joseph Lewis (alias Harris)   *Executed 30th August 1898*

Joseph Lewis (also known as Harris) was convicted of murdering the Margam Estate gamekeeper, Robert Scott, in August 1898. An ex-soldier, Lewis had apparently deserted from the army a few years earlier and was described as being 'the terror of his native place'. He lived and worked in the Aberavon area but the Margam woods were an obvious draw for him.

Lewis was out poaching with several others on that fateful day. The Margam Estate was well known for its stock of game, and Scott was on the lookout for poachers who had been plaguing the area for many months. Despite the potential dangers, Gamekeeper Scott carried only a stick, never a gun.

In a clearing on the estate, Scott chanced upon Joseph Lewis and challenged him. The result was a foregone conclusion: Lewis discharged both barrels of his shotgun into the gamekeeper's head.

Suspicion initially fell upon a man and woman with whom Lewis lodged and they were arrested. Yet the ex-soldier soon gave himself away. One night, he joined a group of colliers who were discussing the murder and, presumably emboldened by beer, made the claim: 'Go on, boys, they've collared the wrong people. It was I who shot Scott.'

If Lewis thought the coal miners would keep his confession to themselves, he was wrong. He was quickly arrested and put on trial. He appeared to have no remorse for the crime, as he was convinced that he was justified in shooting the gamekeeper. *The South Wales Daily Post* reported that Lewis had claimed that:

Scott was a big man and he had a formidable stick. Other poachers had been beaten senseless by keepers. I had a gun to save myself from the same punishment and so I used it.

When he was in prison Lewis found the food not to his liking. He described it as being too scanty and told a friend that he was constantly hungry. Despite this he had for his breakfast, on most occasions, white bread with butter and cheese followed by tea or coffee. For dinner, potatoes, meat, vegetables and bread, and this was followed by the customary small stout allowed, as per instructions for the condemmed man. For his evening meal he usually had meat, salad and bread. His only request was for some bake-stone bread.

On the morning of the execution a crowd of about 3000 assembled outside the prison and numbers were still rising as Warder Williams climbed onto the roof in order to unfurl the black flag. Then, curiously, a boy arrived to deliver milk to the warder's house – he rang the bell timidly, faltered and turned away, unable to cope with the thousands of eyes gazing at him. According to *The South Wales Daily Post*:

> *The warder came to the window and beckoned the lad, no doubt fearful that the lad would go away and not return. The lad appeared to pluck up courage and returned to the gate and delivered the milk, much to the amusement of the onlookers. The lad was seen hurrying away, smiling at this triumph. This little incident tickled the fancy of the crowd who were heard to murmur at the affair, but they all fell into silence as the hour approached.*

James Billington was the executioner, assisted by his son Thomas. They had arrived the

The following poem appeared in The South Wales Daily Post *on 31st August 1989:*

In Margam Wood

Soft lights were in the summer sky,
The air was all perfume,
When Lewis, down the mountain path,
Came walking to his doom.

He turned into the covering wood,
No man can tell his thought,
But on the listening summer air
Was heard the deadly shot.

He fled the spot – he has his gun,
He changed his clothes in vain
For clear behind the avengers came,
He bore the mark of Cain.

And now by law and justice tried
He's numbered with the dead,
For men still keep the olden text,
"Gainst blood unjustly shed'

See passion's work! The summer eve
When calm twilight fell –
A murdered man – a widowed home,
And now, the felon's cell.

'Tis done! The dark death-telling flag
Droops on the conscious air,
His debt to man he now has paid
For his soul we breathe a prayer.

C Westwood

previous day and had the unnerving experience of running into several distraught members of Lewis's family in the Terminus Hotel before the execution. It was, by all accounts, a distressing encounter.

Joseph Lewis walked from his cell to the scaffold, and he seems to have displayed no emotion at all. Death was instantaneous. Out on the roof of the prison Warder Williams unfurled the black flag and the waiting crowd saw it flutter in the breeze.

After the execution, the Billingtons left the prison and walked back to the Terminus Hotel. The crowd had guessed their identities, however, and a huge crowd followed them as they walked. A reporter tried to obtain an interview with the pair but they clearly did not want to speak with him. They later complained to the hotel manager and the young reporter was asked to leave the building.

There are two more interesting footnotes to the execution of Joseph Lewis. Firstly, it seems that he confessed to the murder in a letter to Scott's widow, asking her to forgive him for the crime. There is no record of her response. And secondly, the jurors' fees of twelve shillings each were handed over to *The South Wales Daily Post* to be added to the fund for the relief of distressed people in Cwmbwrla.

Joseph Lewis was buried about twenty yards from the spot where Thomas Nash and Thomas Allen were interred. Like the other executed men, his burial place is marked by a small tablet inset in the prison wall.

This was the last occasion on which the Black Flag was flown from the roof of Swansea Prison. Having come to the conclusion that public executions served no useful purpose, and that they in fact merely played to the morbid urges of a fasinated mob, the authorities decided that in future they would pin a formal notice of the execution to the prison gate once the hanging had taken place.

William Joseph Foy

Executed 8th May 1909

William Foy was an unemployed labourer who lived rough with Mary Ann Rees at the Ynysfach Coke Ovens in Merthyr. On the morning of Christmas Eve 1908, he and Mary Ann had quarrelled, seemingly over another woman.

Foy and Rees had been drinking and Rees, who was known by the nickname Sloppy, stormed out, saying 'All right Joe, I know what it is. It's not me you want, it's Polly Gough.' Foy followed her and later confessed to one of his drinking companions that he had thrown Sloppy down an old shaft at the works.

Not long after this Foy accosted two policemen and asked to be locked up as he had killed Rees:

'I have thrown Sloppy down the hole at the old works,' he said. 'She told me she was going to give me away for living on her prostitution. I've done for her, I'll show you where she is.'

First, a shawl was discovered and then the body of Mary Ann Rees at the bottom of the shaft. Foy was arrested on the spot as there was little or no doubt about his guilt.

At his trial in Cardiff, Foy tried to make some semblance of a defence. He followed Sloppy when she left the room after their quarrel, he said, and in the struggle to induce her to return she slipped and fell

From The South Wales Daily Post, *10th May 1909:*

Merthyr Choir Sings Outside Gaol

A party of choristers from Merthyr (friends and former fellow workmen of the man Foy when he worked at the Plymouth Colliery, Merthyr) arrived at Swansea on the Friday night and sang jovial sacred pieces outside the gaol. Their anxiety to secure a position whereby their former comrade could hear them was intense.

into the hole. It was a poor defence and the guilty verdict was almost inevitable.

The date of the execution was originally set for 20th April, but was postponed due to appeals. These were turned down, with Justice Darling declaring that Foy's act was 'most deliberate and intentional murder'.

The South Wales Daily Post commented that:

> *Foy, during his incarceration in the gaol displayed little emotion, even when his relatives visited him, and discussed football and other topics, spending some time also in improving his handwriting. He received the news of his refusal of commutation with resignation, saying he would meet his fate like a man.*

It is certain that William Joseph Foy meditated deeply on his actions and fate whilst in Swansea Prison. He was baptised into the church by the prison chaplain, and even went so far to state publicly that:

A crowd outside Swansea Prison awaits Foy's execution.
(Courtesy The South Wales Evening Post)

'now that I have been forgiven all my sins, I shall not be afraid to meet God'.

An ex-soldier, Foy was not unfamiliar with death and was determined to make good his promise to die like a man. On one visit made by his father and sister he gave her a religious tract which had been presented to him by the prison chaplain. On the front leaf he had written 'To my beloved sister, Catherine Ann Norbury. My dear sister, learn your dear children what is in this book. Joe, May 5th.' The following week, just prior to his execution, he wrote in a letter to his family: 'I am pleased to tell you that I am going to receive my communion on Friday. I can assure you that, with the help of God, I am quite resigned to my fate, as it is willed by him.'

A letter written from Foy to his sister which appeared in the *South Wales Daily Post*.

Hundreds of people gathered outside the prison on the fateful morning of 8th May. Inside, Foy took everyone by surprise. The *South Wales Daily Post* reporter noted that:

> Foy appeared with a cigarette in his mouth. He held it firmly and was unmistakably smoking, dressed in the evening clothes of a workman, collarless with the neck exposed. He sported a sprig of fern in his

button hole. Foy held himself rigid, with his chest thrown out and to all appeared calm and collected. The only hint or token of wrought feelings was in the wild light in his eyes.

The executioner, Henry Pierrepoint, strapped Foy's legs together and forced the white hood over his head. The cigarette bent but did not break.

When the bolt was drawn, Foy fell six feet and death was instantaneous.

Henry Phillips   *Executed 14th December 1911*

Henry Phillips, a labourer from Gower and a serious alcoholic, lived unhappily with his wife. There were frequent violent quarrels between them and, on more than one occasion, the couple had separated.

Mrs Phillips left the family home for the last time on 13th July 1911, taking her four children with her. She went to stay at her mother's house in Frogmore Lane, Knelston. However, Henry Phillips followed her and, on the morning of 26th July, the couple became involved in a furious row, which culminated in Phillips attacking his wife with a razor outside the house. Mrs Phillips' mother and sister heard pitiful cries of 'Oh Henry, oh Henry', and ran outside. They saw Phillips kneeling on his wife, drawing a razor across her throat. When he saw them, Phillips ran away. The wounded woman was taken to Swansea hospital but later died from her injuries.

The result of the trial was, as expected, a guilty verdict. In *The South Wales Daily Post* it was recorded that:

Phillips, the Gower labourer and doomed man, whilst seated in the docks during the hearing of the evidence, seemed, judging by his demeanour, to accept his fate. Not until the concluding stages of the trial did he show any sign or emotion.

The jury was not long in considering their verdict, and the Judge commended them on their decision to find Phillips guilty – they could not, he said, have done otherwise. On hearing the sentence, Henry Phillips collapsed and had to be escorted from the dock by the warders.

Strenuous efforts were made to have the prisoner reprieved, with supporters arguing that Phillips's plea of insanity had been ignored, and also that the trial had been misdirected by the judge. A petition containing some 7000 signatures was also drawn up, and this was taken to the Home Secretary by John Williams, the MP for Gower. All efforts were in vain, however, and the date of the execution was set for 14th December 1911.

A plate dated 1848 inside the gate of Swansea Prison, which is said to have come from the older prison building which is still standing.

By half past seven in the morning a small crowd had gathered outside the prison gates, braving the cold, damp air and standing in virtual silence as the hour approached. An astute reporter from *The South Wales Daily Post* wrote the following account of the condemned man's last moments:

Attired in the working clothes of an agricultural labourer, he shuffled rather than walked to the gallows, but was in no sense about to collapse. He bore his last few minutes with that same indifference that characterised him at the trial. When he was placed on the trapdoor, the noose already being put round the neck, Phillips turned his head to one side as if to see what was coming next in the carrying out of this grim tragedy of the law, but before he could move again, Ellis had placed the white cap over the head and stepped back.

Outside the gates, three hundred men, women and children saw Principal Warder William Beynon post up a notice on the prison door declaring that Henry Phillips had met his end.

Daniel 'Big Dan' Sullivan   *Executed 6th September 1916*

Known in the town of Dowlais as Big Dan, Sullivan worked as a coker at Dowlais Iron and Steel Works, near Merthyr Tydfil. He was renowned as a heavy drinker and was known for being brutal, violent and very aggressive when he was drunk.

On the night of 8th July 1916, Big Dan had been drinking heavily at the Antelope Inn. When he finally left the pub, he took with him a bottle of rum which the landlord, Daniel Edwards, had sold him. Edwards was later fined £20 and sentenced to 28 days in custody for selling alcohol out of hours.

When he arrived home in the early hours of the morning, Sullivan demanded to know the whereabouts of his wife, Catherine. His stepdaughter, Bridget, told him she was asleep in the bedroom. Sullivan, mad with drink, pulled his wife from her bed, demanding that she make supper, and then proceeded to kick her from the bedroom to the kitchen. A report in the *Merthyr Express* surmises that:

> *The woman must have been unconscious the whole time because she never screamed or made any attempt to defend herself. When the police arrived they found Catherine in a pool of blood on the floor. Sullivan had hid himself in the fowl house.*

The police had been called by Sullivan's stepson, Fred, who ran first to neighbours, but finding no answer there quickly went on to the police station.

On September 2nd, a week before the execution, the Board of Guardians at Merthyr reported that the NSPCC had received from Cork a request that the children go to Ireland to stay with relatives, if the Board was willing to pay the passage. However, the Cork Guardians had reported that the home suggested was not suitable. So the little ones would stay in the care of the Board.*

*as reported in *The Merthyr Express* at the time.

Big Dan Sullivan wore heavy, nailed boots of the type that cokers then wore at the works, and he did terrible damage to his wife. It seems that he literally kicked her to a pulp, her body being bruised, battered and bloodstained from the top of her head to the soles of her feet. Bridget, the stepdaughter, gave evidence at the trial saying that Sullivan had pulled his wife out of the bed and had started to kick her almost at once, saying 'There'll be a corpse leaving the house tonight.' Bridget, who was just nine years old, had fled from the scene.

The jury retired for barely half an hour before returning with a guilty verdict. Big Dan Sullivan commented simply, 'I am not guilty'.

A petition was raised for Sullivan's reprieve but the Home Secretary saw no reason to interfere with the decision of the court. Sullivan was duly executed at nine o'clock in the morning on Wednesday 6th September at Swansea Prison.

He had spent his last night quietly and rose early to receive the last ministrations of Father Eggerton, the Roman Catholic chaplain. He went quietly and with resignation to meet his fate.

Trevor John Edwards   *Executed 11th December 1928*

Trevor Edwards, a collier from Cwmaman, was convicted of murdering his sweetheart Elsie Cook at Llanwenno near Bridgend on 16th June 1928.

Long before he had met Elsie, he had been courting a young woman named Annie Protheroe. Then Annie left Cwmaman to go and live in Swindon, and Edwards had transferred his affections to Elsie Cook. Before long, however, she became pregnant and a distraught Edwards wrote a desperate letter to Annie:

> *Dear Annie,*
> *I am writing to let you know that the trouble I feared has come and by the time that you come home I shall have a wife or a coffin. You might think that I don't think anything of you but you must not think that way because I have never loved anyone else, not in this life.*

Despite having promised to marry Elsie, Trevor Edwards had other plans in mind. On 16th June he took her for a walk on the mountain at Llanwenno, after first calling at a public house and buying a flagon of beer.

At some point during the walk Edwards hit Elsie over the head with the flagon. In his own words:

SENTENCE	Education	Age, Height, and Colour of Hair	TRADE or OCCUPATION	Religion and Birth Place	Nature of Previous Conviction and Reference to last entry	DATE OF DISCHARGE and REMARKS

Handwritten prison records dated 1883.   *(Courtesy H. M. Prison, Swansea)*

61

I smashed the flagon on her head. Fancy that? You would not have believed that her head would have been so hard, but she had a felt hat on. First of all I choked her, but did not choke the life out of her, but into a weakened state. Then I finished her with a razor.

After attempting, and failing, to kill himself, Edwards quickly surrendered to the police and made a full statement, giving the location of Elsie's body. This was duly found, along with an open razor, cigarette ends and the fragments of a broken bottle. The girl's head had been almost severed from her body.

The trial lasted only a day and a guilty verdict was passed. The recommendation of mercy from the jury was ignored and the death sentence given.

Unlike previous executions at Swansea, the trial and hanging of Trevor Edwards did not excite a great deal of interest in the local populace. Edwards had no local connections, beyond the fact that he was tried at Swansea Assizes. Nevertheless, some 200 people turned up on the morning of the execution to keep watch outside the prison gates.

Some interest was expressed at the figure of a lonely, pathetic woman dressed in a fawn coat and black hat who stood by the door until long after eight o'clock. Was it the mother of Trevor

Once a prisoner who has been sentenced to death returns from court, he is placed in a cell for condemned prisoners and is watched night and day by two officers. Amenities such as cards, chess, dominoes and so on are provided in the cell and the officers are encouraged to – in fact, invariably do – join the prisoner in these games. Newspapers and books are also provided. Food is provided from the main kitchens, the prisoner being placed on a hospital diet with such additions as the Medical Officers thinks advisable. A pint of beer or stout is supplied daily, on request, and ten cigarettes or half an ounce of pipe tobacco are allowed unless medical reasons prohibit it. The prisoner may smoke in his cell as well as on exercise.

Edwards? As it happened, she had no connection with the condemned man, but was a member of the public who was waiting for her son who was due to be released from prison that day. His discharge had been delayed until after the execution.

The near fatal accident to one of the executioners on that day attracted almost as much attention as the condemned man's fate. *The South Wales Daily Post* reported that:

> *Baxter was the hangman, and was assisted by Alfred Allen. Allen was a new assistant, at what was his first execution. Baxter was very quick in placing the noose and pulling the lever. Allen was not so quick, and when the drop opened Allen followed Edwards into the pit. No blame was attached; it was claimed by the Governor to be a mixture of the hangman's alacrity and Allen's slightly defective vision.*

The assistant was unhurt and Edwards died instantly. To the end he had, apparently, displayed no emotion and had maintained a stoical calm. At 8.14 a.m., the following notice was posted on the prison door:

> *Declaration of the Sheriff and Others*
> *We, the undersigned, hereby declare that judgement of death was this day executed on Trevor John Edwards, in His Majesty's Prison, Swansea, in our presence.*
> *Eleventh December 1928*
> (signed)   *Theodore Gibbins, Sheriff of Glamorgan*
> *T. Brown, Governor of Swansea Prison*
> *J. H. Watkin-Jones, Chaplain to Swansea Prison*

Rex Harvey Jones and
Robert Thomas Mackintosh   *Executed 4th August 1949*

The execution of two men from the Port Talbot/Neath area on 4th August 1949 was unusual in that the hangings were carried out simultaneously, and side by side. It was the only such execution at Swansea where the crimes were unrelated and it was the first joint execution in the prison since that of the two Greek sailors in 1858.

The South Wales Daily Post was struck by the similarity of the men's crimes:

> *Only two days separated the two death dramas. It was on Saturday morning of June 4th that the body of 16-year-old Beryl Beechey, slain by Robert Thomas Mackintosh, was found on the railway embankment in Port Talbot.*
>
> *The initial sense of horror was at its full height when, on the morning of June 6th, came the news that the body of another girl, Beatrice May Watts, aged 20, of Abercregan, had been found in a plantation, and that Rex Harvey Jones had surrendered to the police and confessed.*

Rex Harvey Jones was a young man who lived in Dyffryn Rhondda. On the evening of 6th June 1949 he and his brother were drinking in a club in Neath. That same evening, Beatrice Watts (known as Peggy) went to a canteen dance in Morriston. Afterwards, by pure chance, Jones and Peggy met in Victoria Gardens in Neath and travelled home by the same bus.

The bus was crowded and, it seems, Peggy Watts sat on Jones's lap for the journey. Just before eleven they arrived in Dyffryn Rhondda and Jones told his brother that he was going to walk the girl home.

They had known each other for a few months and Rex Harvey Jones was last seen walking in the direction of the girl's house, his arm around her shoulders.

Early the following morning Jones telephoned the police, saying, 'I have killed a girl, I've killed Peggy Watts.' He told them where to find the body, saying that they had had sexual intercourse and that he then killed her. He could not explain why. *The South Wales Daily Post* takes up the tale:

> *The police officer did not take the motorcar but went on his bicycle. On the way there he saw Jones walking along the road and asked him, 'Are you the man who telephoned?' He replied, 'I am.' He was cautioned and said, 'I have strangled Peggy Watts with my hands. I felt her pulse and it had stopped. I smothered the girl in the woods. We had intimacy first.*

Jones directed the policeman to the place where he had left the body. Extensive bruising in the region of her neck indicated that considerable force must have been used.

Jones pleaded not guilty to the charge of murder when his trial began at Glamorgan Assizes in Swansea. The Judge told the jury to 'steel your hearts against the strain of good character, steel your hearts in order to see that justice is done,' and in due course a guilty verdict was returned.

The second south Wales murder which took place that June was committed by Robert Thomas Mackintosh. On the evening of 3rd June Beryl Beechey, aged just sixteen years old, was sent on a message to the Mackintosh's house in Vivian Street, Aberavon. Mrs Mackintosh was out, and only her son Robert was at home.

A straitjacket.

The girl did not return home, however, and shortly after six o'clock the following morning her body was discovered lying on a railway embankment on the other side of the road from where Robert Mackintosh lived. A thick cord had been tied twice around her neck. A post mortem showed that she had been sexually assaulted, that she had been a virgin before the assault and that considerable violence had been used.

When questioned by police, Mackintosh admitted that the girl had come to his home but, when she realised that his sister, June, was not there, she had left, and he had carried on with the housework he had started before her arrival:

> *The police carried out an examination of the house and revealed a black patch which turned out to be blood under the bed. Other marks of blood were discovered in other parts of the house and in the kitchen. Asked by the police to account for the blood under the bed, his first explanation was that he had cut his toe.*

It was enough to warrant further questioning and Mackintosh soon admitted that only a few months previously, 'I had a blackout and tried to kiss my sister June. We were in the house and I caught hold of her a bit rough and my father threatened to give me a good lacing.'

Shortly afterwards he confessed to the murder. In his own words:

> *We were talking for a few minutes, then something came over me, I don't remember what. The next thing I remember was that I was in bed and Beryl was half under the bed. I realised that I had done something wrong but what it was I did not know, and that was well into the night. I had no intention of doing it; I did not want to do it. The first thing I could see was Beryl dead in the bedroom, partly underneath the bed.*

Mackintosh carried the dead girl downstairs, put a coat across her body and took her outside. He then threw the body over the wall onto the railway embankment. It was, he said, 'the same as happened before, when I tried to get across my sister.'

Robert Mackintosh admitted his guilt and was duly sentenced to death for the crime.

Serious attempts were made to obtain reprieves for the two young men but to no effect. The execution date was set for Thursday 4th August. Swansea had suffered much excitement and been badly damaged by enemy bombing during the Second World War but, even so, the thought of a double execution aroused considerable interest in the town. Several hundred people waited outside the prison as the appointed hour approached. At 9.15 a.m. two warders emerged from the main prison door, removed the notices of execution, and replaced them with four statements declaring that the hangings had been carried out. Swansea's last double execution was over.

Albert Jenkins   *Executed 19th April 1950*

On 21st March 1950, the Rosemarket farmer Albert Edward Jenkins was convicted of killing his landlord, William Llewellyn. The jury at the Pembrokeshire Assizes, consisting of ten men and two women, took less than two hours to reach their verdict.

Throughout the trial Jenkins had denied the allegation. The facts of the case, however, were clear.

On the morning of 10th October 1949, Jenkins was visited by his landlord at his home, Lower Furze Hill Farm, in Rosemarket, Pembrokeshire. There was back rent to pay and discussions were also taking place regarding Jenkins buying the farm. He claimed to have given Llewellyn £1,050 that day: £50 for the rent, and the rest in order to purchase the farm. The money was taken from a roof beam where he had stored it. William Llewellyn never returned home and his wife subsequently alerted the police. His body was found the next day, buried in a clay pit on Jenkin's land. The injuries to the body were dreadful, revealing that he had been killed by a number of cruelly heavy blows.

According to *The South Wales Evening Post*, the Judge pointed out to the jury that

> *there was no evidence, no evidence of any eyewitnesses, but from the knowledge of affairs the jury would hardly expect in murder cases to find eyewitnesses. The evidence placed before them by the Crown was circumstantial and circumstantial evidence was often the best.*

The case for the prosecution was that Llewellyn was killed by Albert Jenkins. Despite what the accused man said about giving his landlord a considerable sum of money – and having a receipt to prove that the money did, indeed, pass hands – no cash was ever found on the body.

An officer of the Milk Marketing Board, Mr Cudd, had called at Lower Furze Hill Farm on the morning of 10th October and saw Albert Jenkins driving his tractor down the field. There was, he said, a large bundle on the box of the tractor, covered by a tarpaulin, and Jenkins 'looked rather wild'.

Llewellyn's bicycle – on which he had arrived at the farm – was later found at nearby Neyland. Two witnesses claimed that they had seen Jenkins riding a bicycle towards Neyland on the afternoon of 10th October, yet when he was later seen by a local policeman, returning from Pembroke Fair, he was walking and there was no sign of the bicycle.

William Llewellyn's boots were also discovered under manure in the calves' cot on the farm, and leather laces on the dead man matched two more laces found on Jenkins. Earth taken from in front of Jenkin's house was, when tested, found to be saturated with human blood.

The prosecution case was clear. After obtaining a receipt for the money, Jenkins had clubbed the unlucky Llewellyn to death and reclaimed his money. He had then covered Llewellyn's body with a tarpaulin and taken it to the clay pit for burial. When the guilty verdict was given, Albert Jenkins gazed intently at the Judge and remained unmoved during the proceedings.

Jenkins was executed on the morning of 19th April 1950, with executioner Albert Pierrepoint officiating. At 9.25 a.m. the main gate of Swansea Prison opened and two warders posted the declaration of the sheriff and a certificate from the surgeon on the door. A crowd of about thirty-five local people stood outside the prison.

Ronald Lewis Harries

Executed 28th April 1954

The case of Ronald Lewis Harries aroused great interest in the county of Carmarthenshire, and in the county town itself, when he appeared at the Carmarthen Assizes on 16th March 1954.:

> *Harries sat in the dock with arms folded. He wore a navy blue suit, white shirt and collar and a maroon tie, and he had a white handkerchief in his breast pocket.*
>
> *Crush barriers of trestle-tables and rope were erected overnight on both sides of the street outside the Shire Hall. A queue was formed at 3.30 a.m. and many of the people had blankets and flasks of tea. Among the early arrivals were relatives who had come from a village 13 miles away.*

Ronald Harries, who was aged twenty-six, lived at Ashwell Farm in Pendine. He was charged with the murder of John Harries, a distant relative from Derlwyn Farm, Llanginning, whose body – along with that of his wife Phoebe – was unearthed from a shallow grave in a field at Cadno Farm, the home of Ronald Harries's parents. Despite the discovery of two bodies, Harries was only tried for one murder, as *The South Wales Evening Post* explained:

> *It is the practice of the courts that if a man is charged with the murder of two persons, he is never tried for both murders together. The prosecution always proceeds with one charge alone.*

The facts of the case were a little confusing. Sometime between 8.00 p.m. on Friday 16th October and 16th November 1953, John Harries and his wife vanished from their home. The prosecution alleged that the disappearance had actually occurred that first Friday night. What is certain is that there had been no sighting of the couple after they returned to their home from a chapel thanksgiving service on 15th October.

The investigation was conducted by Superintendent John Capstick of New Scotland Yard. As a matter of routine he interviewed Ronald Harries at the police station in St Clears and was far from happy with the man's answers to his questions. Harries was evasive and contradictory in his statements and immediately became a suspect.

> ## The Fatal 16th
>
> The sixteenth day of the month had a special significance in the case of Ronald Harries.
>
> ### October 16th
> John and Phoebe Harries vanish from Derlwyn Farm.
>
> ### November 16th
> The bodies of John and Phoebe Harries are unearthed from a field of kale at Cadno Farm.
>
> ### March 16th
> Ronald Harries is sentenced to death for the murder of his 'uncle'.

Although the accused man was only distantly related to John and Phoebe Harries, he had always referred to them as 'Uncle and Aunt'. Harries insisted that he had driven the couple to Carmarthen Station on the morning of Saturday 16th October, on the first stage of their journey to London where, he claimed, they had gone for a holiday. Yet relatives of the missing couple were adamant that this had not happened – they had not taken any holidays for twenty years, they claimed, and would not have done so without first informing family and friends of their intentions.

There were many other concerns about Ronald Harries. To start with, he had taken the cows from his uncle's farm soon after the disappearance and was known to covet the stock, implements and property of Derlwyn Farm. And in the days after the disappearance his Land Rover was seen constantly driving to and from the farm.

An intensive three-week search of the area was begun, with hundreds of local people joining in to help. Then, on 16th November, police uncovered the bodies of John and Phoebe Harries, buried in a field of kale at Cadno Farm. They had been killed by repeated blows from a circular blunt instrument about one and a quarter inches in diameter. Harries possessed just such a hammer and, that evening, he was arrested and charged with the murder.

When the guilty verdict was passed, Harries continued to protest his innocence. Nevertheless, it was reported that:

> *When Harries left the Shire at 6.15 p.m. handcuffed to a prison warder, the crowd generally booed him, though some sections were cheering. As he entered the taxi he smiled at the crowd and, as it drove off, raised his hand to acquaintances standing nearby.*

Harries was executed at Swansea on 28th April 1954, after a crowd of around 150 turned up to hold vigil outside the prison doors. Despite having been somewhat blasé after his conviction, it seems that Harries collapsed when executioners Pierrepoint and Robert Stewart arrived at his cell, and had to be assisted to the gallows.

Vivian Frederick Teed   *Executed 6th May 1958*

The last execution ever to be held at Swansea Prison was that of Vivian Frederick Teed on Tuesday 6th May 1958.

Teed was convicted of murdering 73-year-old William Williams, a sub-postmaster at Fforestfach, Swansea. Williams lived alone in the Carmarthen Road Post Office which he had run for many years. Teed knew the premises well, having been one of the builders who carried out alterations on the premises earlier in the year.

Recently, Teed had been out of work and was in urgent need of money. He was living with a woman from Limeslade but, in late October 1957, she was admitted to hospital where she suffered a miscarriage. At about this same time, Teed met a man called Ronald Williams at a cafe in Cwmbwrla and told him that he had a 'job' planned at the Fforestfach Post office. Teed had a long criminal record for damage to property, theft and assault. He had already served two years' imprisonment and during his time in the RAF had been absent without leave on many occasions. He was, it was reported, impulsively aggressive and was at various times, abusive, sentimental, jealous and indifferent.

Teed chose the night of 15th November to rob the Post Office. He knocked at the side door, not really expecting an answer. He had seen no lights from inside but thought that he had better check, just in case. To his surprise Mr Williams answered the knock. According to *The South Wales Evening Post*:

> *Pushing his way in he struck Mr Williams . . . In an alleged statement Teed had said that he had used a hammer which was in his pocket. This was of significance as there were no less than 27 separate wounds on Williams's head. Some of these had been inflicted with such violence that the bones of the skull had been forced into the brain and the shaft of the hammer had broken.*

The money from the Post Office was locked in the safe and Teed left with nothing to show for his efforts. Later that night, he admitted to Ronald Williams that he had 'done the job' and had hit the postmaster.

He also commented that he had probably left his fingerprints all over the place and had left the hammer at the scene of the crime.

At first Teed denied being near the Post Office when the police questioned him. Later, however, he admitted to the break-in and the assault. There was considerable debate about the killer's psychological state, with the defence arguing that the crime took place when Teed was suffering from 'an abnormality of the mind which impaired his mental responsibility'. The jury at the trial returned to the court room three times, being unable to reach a verdict, only to be directed to retire again each time to reconsider the evidence. Finally, a verdict of guilty was returned.

Teed was executed on 6th May 1958, following the failure of an appeal to the Home Secretary. Under the new rule, no notices were pinned to the main gates of Swansea Prison to announce that the execution had taken place.

It was a rainy morning, and at the appointed hour only a few men and women were waiting outside the gates, but residents of nearby streets were to be seen standing in their doorways, waiting for the final moment.

The chaplain of Swansea Prison, Reverend Leslie Norman, later said of Teed:

> *He wasn't a murderer – he killed a man. If you told him that he was going to murder someone, he would have been shocked. He was caught in the act. They fought and one died. He had no intention of murdering him.*

Conclusion

With the execution of Vivian Frederick Teed, executions at Swansea Prison came to an end. He was the last man ever to go to the gallows in Swansea.

It was another seven years before the death penalty was finally abolished, with the last execution in Britain taking place in 1964. The execution shed at Swansea Prison has now gone, and workshops and instruction areas mark the place where condemned men once spent their last moments.

The rights or wrongs of the system and process of capital punishment have been the subject of much debate over the years, as is clear from discussion of the Swansea executions as they were

Swansea Prison's oldest building, which dates from 1848.

reported in the local press at the time. Capital punishment has continued to exercise the minds of those in authority throughout the twentieth century. Suffice to say that for many years it was a part of the history of these islands. And it is clear from accounts of executions at Swansea Prison that this was a penal institution which played a full and active part in that history.

A prison landing at Swansea.

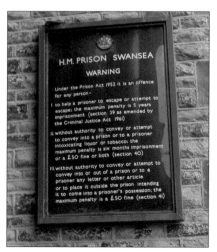

The notice at the entrance to Swansea Prison.

Select Bibliography

Books

Fielding, Steve, *The Hangman's Record, 1868-1899*, Vol. I (Chancery House Press, 1994)

Fielding, Steve, *The Hangman's Record, 1900-1929*, Vol. II (Chancery House Press, 1995)

Hunt, W. W. (Superintendent), *To Serve My People* (by kind permission of Rev. Ted Hunt, retired chaplain of Swansea Prison)

Pierrepoint, Albert, *Executioner Pierrepoint: The Amazing Autobiography of the World's Most Famous Executioner* (Coronet Books; Hodder and Stoughton, 1974)

Webb, Harri, *Collected Poems*, edited by Meic Stephens (Gomer Press, 1995)

Newspapers

The Cambrian
The South Wales Daily Post
The South Wales Evening Post
The Merthyr Express
The Western Mail